Aye-Ayes

Victoria Blakemore

Copyright info/picture credits

Table of Contents

What Are Aye-Ayes?

Aye-ayes are a special kind of mammal called a primate. Apes and monkeys are also primates. Aye-ayes are also **classified** as a kind of lemur.

They have very thin black fur. Some people think that aye-ayes look like rats.

Aye-ayes are known for their

bright yellow or orange eyes.

Size

An adult aye-aye's body can grow to be up to eighteen inches long. Their tail can be up to two feet long.

Although they have a long body and tail, aye-ayes do not weigh much. They usually weigh less than four pounds.

Physical Characteristics

Aye-ayes have a long, fluffy tail. It helps them to balance as they run through the trees.

Their dark fur works as **camouflage**. It helps them to blend in to the trees at night. They can be very hard to see.

Aye-ayes have very large ears for an animal of their size. This allows them to hear insects and grubs through tree bark. 7

Habitat

Aye-ayes live in the rainforest.

It is very warm and wet there.

There are lots of trees and plants.

They stay up high in trees. This helps them to stay safe from predators. It also means that they are not seen very often by humans.

Range

Aye-ayes are only found in the

rainforests of Madagascar.

Madagascar is a large island

off the coast of Africa.

Diet

Aye-ayes are **omnivores**. They eat both meat and plants.

Their diet is made up of fruit, insects, nectar from flowers, plants, and fungi. A lot of their diet is made up of insect grubs.

The word grubs is another word

for some insect larvae. They are

often found in holes in trees.

To find food, aye-ayes tap on trees and listen for the sound of a **hollow** spot.

Once they find a hollow area, they stick their long, thin finger inside. They use it to pull insects out of holes in tree bark.

Aye-ayes have an unusual hand.

It has five fingers, but their middle

finger is very long and thin.

Communication

Aye-ayes use mainly sound

and scent to communicate

with each other.

Each aye-aye has a special

scent that they use to mark

their **territory**. For most of the

year, aye-ayes share their

territory with other aye-ayes.

Aye-ayes can make several
different sounds. They can
scream, hiss, and whimper.

Movement

Aye-ayes are very **agile**. They are able to run and jump from tree branch to tree branch.

Their long claws and paws that are like hands help them to grip tree branches as they climb.

Aye-ayes are **arboreal**. They spend almost all of their time in the trees.

Young Aye-ayes

Aye-ayes usually have one

baby. Their babies are

called infants.

Infant aye-ayes are silver

with a dark stripe down their

back. They will change to a

darker color as they get

older.

Young aye-ayes have even
thinner fur than their parents. It
gets thicker over time.

Aye-aye Life

Aye-ayes are **solitary**

animals. They spend most

of their time alone.

They are not seen with other

aye-ayes very often.

Aye-ayes do not **groom**

each other like most

primates do.

Aye-ayes are **nocturnal**. They
are most active at night.

Bad Luck

In parts of Madagascar, aye-ayes are thought to bring bad luck.

This **superstition** has caused many people to kill aye-ayes if they see them. The belief is that killing them is the only way to prevent bad luck.

Many years ago, people would
leave their homes if an aye-aye
was seen nearby. Whole villages
were left abandoned.

25

Population

Aye-ayes are **endangered**.
There are not many left in the
wild.

In the 1950's, they were
thought to be **extinct**.
Aye-ayes hadn't been seen in
the wild in several years.

In the wild, aye-ayes can live

up to twenty years.

Aye-Ayes in Danger

Aye-ayes face two main threats: habitat loss and being hunted.

For many years, aye-ayes were killed because they were thought to bring bad luck. This caused their population to **decline**.

Aye-aye habitats are destroyed

to make space for more

buildings and farmland.

Helping Aye-Ayes

Places like the Duke Lemur Center are trying to help aye-ayes survive. They are releasing aye-ayes into the wild to try to help the population increase.

In Madagascar, laws have been passed to protect aye-ayes from being hunted.

There are special protected areas in Madagascar. They provide animals like aye-ayes with a safe habitat to live in.

People are trying to educate others about aye-ayes. They hope that people will want to help aye-ayes if they know about their problems.

Glossary

Agile: able to move quickly and gracefully

Arboreal: an animal that lives in the trees

Camouflage: using color to blend in to the surroundings

Classified: grouped, ordered

Decline: get smaller

Endangered: at risk of becoming extinct

Extinct: when there are no more of an animal left in the wild

Groom: to make clean and neat in appearance

Hollow: having an empty space inside

Nocturnal: animals that are active and night

Omnivore: an animal that eats meat and plants

Solitary: living alone

Superstition: a belief that is not based on fact

Territory: an area of land that an animal claims as its own

About the Author

Victoria Blakemore is a first grade

teacher in Southwest Florida with a

passion for reading.

You can visit her at

www.elementaryexplorers.com

Also in This Series

Gray Wolves	Sloths	Flamingos	Camels	Koalas	Honey Bees	Pandas
Pangolins	White-Tailed Deer	Orcas	Giraffes	Corn	Meerkats	Echidnas
Walruses	Raccoons	Bald Eagles	Apples	Arctic Foxes	Red Pandas	Cassowaries
Tigers	Ladybugs	Moose	Beluga Whales	Leopards	Elephants	Jellyfish
Binturongs	Lions	Dolphins	Reindeer	Hammerhead Sharks	Hippos	Pumpkins
Peafowl	Chameleons	Florida Panthers	Aye-Ayes	Black Bears	Cheetahs	Manatees
Gingerbread	Polar Bears	Hot Chocolate	Orangutans	Coyotes	Marshmallows	Strawberries

Also in This Series

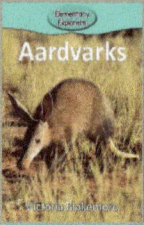

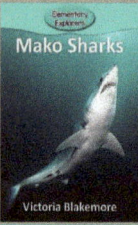

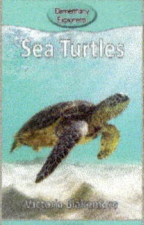

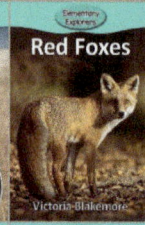

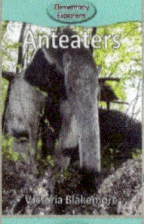

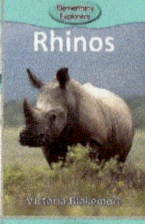

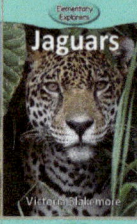

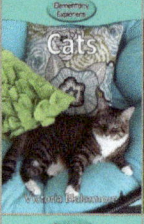

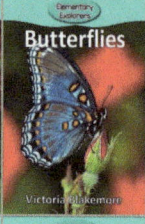

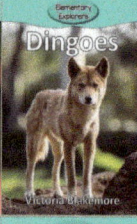

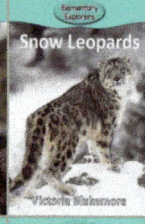

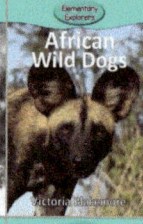

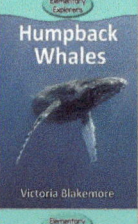

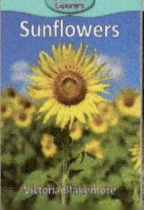

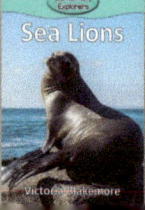

Aardvarks	Mako Sharks	Alligators	Frogs	Hedgehogs	Brown Bears	Bongos
Sea Turtles	Quokkas	Muskrats	Zebras	Red Foxes	Ring-Tailed Lemurs	Platypuses
Anteaters	Kangaroos	Rhinos	Jaguars	Wombats	Capybaras	Gorillas
Cats	Skunks	Butterflies	Dingoes	Snow Leopards	African Wild Dogs	Penguins
Whale Sharks	Wolverines	Warthogs	Caracals	Badgers	Seals	Hummingbirds
Pikas	Humpback Whales	Pumas	Lemonade	Llamas	Tulips	Ostriches
Sunflowers	Fennec Foxes	Sea Lions	Squirrels	Roses	Porcupines	Ice Cream

www.ingramcontent.com/pod-product-compliance
Lightning Source LLC
Chambersburg PA
CBHW051250020426
42333CB00025B/3145